The Writing of "The Star-Spangled Banner"

Sabrina Crewe and Scott Ingram

Gareth Stevens Publishing

A WORLD ALMANAC EDUCATION GROUP COMPANY

Please visit our web site at: www.garethstevens.com
For a free color catalog describing Gareth Stevens Publishing's list of high-quality
books and multimedia programs, call 1-800-542-2595 (USA) or 1-800-387-3178
(Canada). Gareth Stevens Publishing's fax: (414) 332-3567.

Library of Congress Cataloging-in-Publication Data

Crewe, Sabrina.
    The writing of "The Star-Spangled Banner" / by Sabrina Crewe and Scott Ingram.
        p. cm. — (Events that shaped America)
    Includes bibliographical references and index.
    ISBN 0-8368-3409-7 (lib. bdg.)
    1. Baltimore, Battle of, Baltimore, Md., 1814—Juvenile literature. 2. United States—
History—War of 1812—Flags—Juvenile literature. 3. Flags—United States—History—
19th Century—Juvenile literature. 4. Key, Francis Scott, 1779-1843—Juvenile literature.
5. Star-spangled banner (Song)—Juvenile literature. I. Ingram, Scott. II. Title.
III. Series.
    E356.B2C74 2004
    973.5'23'0975271—dc22   2004045266

This North American edition first published in 2005 by
Gareth Stevens Publishing
A World Almanac Education Group Company
330 West Olive Street, Suite 100
Milwaukee, WI 53212 USA

This edition © 2005 by Gareth Stevens Publishing.

Produced by Discovery Books
Editor: Sabrina Crewe
Designer and page production: Sabine Beaupré
Photo researcher: Sabrina Crewe
Maps and diagrams: Stefan Chabluk
Gareth Stevens editor: Jim Mezzanotte
Gareth Stevens art direction: Tammy West
Gareth Stevens production: Jessica Morris

Photo credits: Corbis: cover, pp. 9, 15, 16, 18, 19, 20, 21, 22, 26; The Granger Collection:
p. 23; Maryland Historical Society: p. 5; North Wind Picture Archives: pp. 4, 7, 8, 10, 11,
12, 13, 14, 24, 25; Smithsonian Institution National Museum of American History: p. 27.

Printed in the United States of America

1 2 3 4 5 6 7 8 9 09 08 07 06 05 04

Contents

In September 1814, Francis Scott Key wrote a poem called "The Defense of Fort McHenry." The words of that poem are now the lyrics of the U.S. national anthem.

The British Attack Begins

Heavy rain fell on Fort McHenry in the second week of September 1814. The star-shaped fort lay in Chesapeake Bay, at the southern end of the Patapsco River in Maryland. The fort's purpose was to protect the busy port of Baltimore from the British army.

Britain had been fighting the United States for two years in a war now known as the War of 1812. By early September, more than thirty British ships were on the Patapsco River, getting ready to attack Baltimore. On September 13, 1814, the cannons on board the British ships began to fire exploding **shells** toward Fort McHenry.

Under Siege

The British bombardment continued for more than twenty-four hours, but the Americans inside the fort held their ground. In a later report, Fort McHenry's commander, Major George Armistead, wrote that despite "a constant and tremendous shower of shells . . . not a man shrunk from the conflict."

A Witness

Several miles away, an American lawyer named Francis Scott Key heard the bombardment and feared the defeat of Fort McHenry. On the morning of September 14, however, Key saw that a huge United States flag was still flying over the fort. Inspired by the sight, Key composed a poem, and its words later became the lyrics to "The Star-Spangled Banner." Because of the song, the defense of Fort McHenry will always be remembered in American history.

An Important Battle

The British attack on Fort McHenry and the fort's defense by the United States is known as the Battle of Baltimore. The capture of Baltimore could well have spelled defeat for the United States. By standing up to the British bombardment, however, the soldiers at Fort McHenry disrupted the British plan to invade Baltimore. The attacking force had to retreat from Chesapeake Bay and—soon afterward—from U.S. territory to the north as well.

These soldiers fought in the Battle of Baltimore in 1814. They were photographed in 1880 on Defenders' Day, which is celebrated every year in Baltimore.

Chapter One

Trouble with Britain

Trade and Shipping

In the early 1800s, the United States had a flourishing trade with Europe. North America was rich in natural resources and had many products—such as cotton, tobacco, and grain—that Europeans wanted. On the Atlantic and Pacific Oceans, U.S. **merchant ships** were the main carriers of goods to Europe from the Americas, the West Indies, and Asia. For these reasons, American shipping and trade was very important to two large European powers, France and Britain.

When these nations fought with each other, which they did for many years between 1793 and 1814, U.S. ships and goods got caught in the middle. This happened because both

This map shows U.S. territories and states in the early 1800s. It also shows the parts of North America that belonged to Spain and Britain.

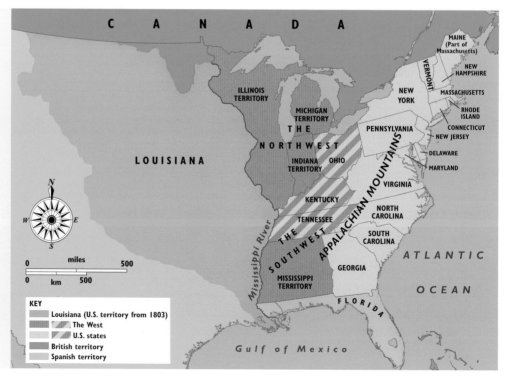

KEY
- Louisiana (U.S. territory from 1803)
- The West
- U.S. states
- British territory
- Spanish territory

6

In the early 1800s, thousands of American sailors were kidnapped by the British navy.

nations decided a good way to hurt the other side was to deny it access to U.S. goods, and so they targeted U.S. ships.

Seizing Ships and Sailors

The navies of Britain and France patrolled the seas to keep vessels out of each other's ports. The British navy was by far the most powerful, and it was Britain that seized most ships, greatly damaging the U.S. **economy**. Britain's actions made U.S. leaders, merchants, and shippers very angry.

The British had another bad practice at sea. They kidnapped sailors from American vessels, claiming the men

North America in the Early 1800s

In the early 1800s, the United States of America was a new nation and not nearly as big as it is now. The original thirteen states and Vermont—which became a state in 1791—were all in the East. The United States also controlled the territory between the United States and the Mississippi River, an area called simply "the **West**." The United States claimed the Louisiana Territory as well, bought from France in 1803. The rest of North America was divided between Britain and Spain. Britain controlled Canada and several islands in the West Indies. Spain controlled Florida and everything west of the Louisiana Territory.

were escaped British sailors, and forced them into the British navy. Some of the sailors had indeed run away from the British navy because of brutal conditions, but most of the kidnapped sailors were Americans. The kidnappings, known as "impressment," infuriated Americans.

The Embargo Act

President Thomas Jefferson knew that the U.S. Army and Navy were no match for the British. So instead of declaring war over Britain's bullying behavior at sea, he ordered all British warships to stay out of U.S. waters. Then, when impressment continued, Congress passed the **Embargo** Act in December 1807. The law closed U.S. ports to foreign ships and prevented American ships from sailing to foreign ports.

In 1809, however, Congress **repealed** the Embargo Act because it was hurting the U.S.

The Embargo Act stopped Americans from selling their goods legally, so they started smuggling. This cartoon shows a tobacco exporter caught in the act of smuggling tobacco to British ships.

economy more than anything else. Goods were sitting in warehouses. Crops were rotting. Sailors, dockworkers, and laborers were out of work.

Henry Clay was the leader of the War Hawks in Congress. He remained a powerful force in U.S. politics for many years after the War of 1812.

The War Hawks

In 1809, when James Madison became president, resentment against Britain was growing. It wasn't just because of Britain's actions at sea. Americans wanted the British out of Canada, too. In 1811, a group of congressmen, the War Hawks, made fierce speeches calling for an invasion of Canada. The War Hawks claimed that the British there were helping Native American tribes attack U.S. settlers in the **Northwest**.

The Right of Occupancy

"The white people have no right to take the land from the Indians, because they had it first; it is theirs. . . . All red men have equal rights to the unoccupied land. The right of occupancy . . . belongs to the first who sits down on his blanket or skins which he has thrown upon the ground; and till he leaves it no other has a right."

Letter from Tecumseh, leader of Native resistance to white settlement, to William Henry Harrison, governor of Indiana Territory, 1811

Conflict in the West

The conflict between Native Americans and U.S. settlers had been almost constant in the first decade of the 1800s, as more and more white settlers moved into the West. The governors of western territories aggressively attempted to get rid of Native Americans. Between 1802 and 1805, some tribes living in areas that are now part of Indiana, Wisconsin, and Illinois were tricked into selling their land. Others were forcibly removed, and many were killed.

Bitter feelings grew on both sides. To complicate things further, the British provided food, clothing, and weapons to Native Americans in an attempt to support the tribes and so prevent U.S. expansion into Canada. As the conflict increased, Americans saw the British as a challenge to U.S. growth.

Settlers in the Northwest, such as this family in Ohio, took over Native American homelands in the 1800s.

The War Hawks helped spread a wave of anti-British feeling across the country. They declared the right of the United States to expand into Canada and even talked about taking control of Florida from Spain. Not surprisingly, these ideas appealed to the War Hawks' southern and western supporters, who were hungry for more land.

James Madison was president of the United States during the War of 1812. He was reluctant to start a war but eventually gave in to pressure from the War Hawks.

War Is Declared

On June 1, 1812, President Madison sent a document to Congress that listed all U.S. complaints against Britain. The list mentioned impressment, the searching of U.S. vessels in U.S. waters, embargoes that harmed the U.S. economy, and the alliance between Native Americans and the British army. On June 18, 1812, Congress declared war on Britain, and the War of 1812 began.

Dreaded Enemy

"Of all the enemies to [the] public . . . war, is, perhaps, the most to be dreaded."

James Madison, Political Observations, *1795*

Chapter Two

The War of 1812

Fighting Chances

The United States was not prepared for war. There were fewer than seven thousand soldiers in the U.S. Army, and the U.S. Navy was small. The local **militia** units were largely untrained.

Tecumseh (c.1768–1836)

Tecumseh, a Shawnee warrior, began his resistance to white settlement in the 1790s. In the early 1800s, Tecumseh formed a **confederation** of Native American tribes in an attempt to stop white settlement in the West. When the War of 1812 began, Tecumseh and his confederation joined forces with the British, and Tecumseh led thousands of Native Americans into battle against the United States.

A hero to his people and famed as an honorable warrior, Tecumseh was killed at the Battle of the Thames in Canada in October 1813.

Tecumseh confronts William Henry Harrison, governor of Indiana, about white settlement on Native homelands.

Native American military forces attack the U.S. post Fort Dearborn, near present-day Chicago, in August 1812.

On the other side, the British had the most powerful navy in the world. In addition, their army was helped by Native Americans who had taken Britain's side, hoping to keep American settlers off their lands.

Defeats and Victories

By summer of 1812, the British and their Indian allies had captured many U.S. forts, and Britain controlled most of the Northwest. British forces moved east, where they burned Buffalo, New York, and captured part of Maine.

The United States, however, destroyed the Canadian capital of York on Lake Ontario in April 1813. The U.S. Navy also performed well on the Great Lakes. In one dramatic naval battle in September 1813, a U.S. **fleet** won control of Lake Erie.

A Sickening Sight
"We witnessed a sight which made my heart sick within me. . . . The [soldiers] . . . were marched like cattle . . . guarded by troops with all the parade and pomp of British insolence, and we . . . could only look on and sicken at the sight."

War Hawk Peter B. Porter, describing defeated U.S. troops marching along the Niagara River, September 1812

The Situation Gets Worse

Even after several victories, many Americans were becoming disillusioned with the war. One newspaper called the War of 1812 "an unbroken series of disasters, disgrace, ruin and death." To make matters worse, a British **blockade** in the East was cutting off supplies. Then, in the spring of 1814, a fleet of British warships carrying more than fifteen thousand new troops was sent to the United States.

Landing in Maryland

On August 19, 1814, a force of almost 4,500 British soldiers sailed up Chesapeake Bay and landed at Benedict, Maryland, on the Patuxent River. From there, the troops marched northwest toward Washington, D.C., about 60 miles (100 kilometers) away. They planned to destroy Washington, D.C., to retaliate for the burning of the Canadian capital at York. Then they would attack Baltimore.

British ships form a blockade in Chesapeake Bay during the War of 1812. Their presence prevented U.S. warships from sailing.

Sound of the Cannon

"Will you believe it, my sister? We have had a battle, or skirmish, near Bladensburg, and here I am still, within sound of the cannon! Mr. Madison comes not. May God protect us! "

First Lady Dolley Madison, in a letter to her sister as the British approached Washington, August 24, 1814

The British Attack Washington, D.C.

The British collided with a U.S. force on August 24, 1814, in the Battle of Bladensburg. British troops quickly overwhelmed the American resistance and reached Washington, D.C., the same evening. They invaded the stone Capitol building, where they piled up

shutters and doors and started a huge bonfire. The Treasury building was burned next. From there, the troops invaded the President's mansion—known today as the White House—and set fire to it.

Chesapeake Bay is about 200 miles (320 km) long and 35 miles (56 km) across at its widest part. The bay is very shallow in places, which made it difficult for large British warships to get close to Baltimore in the invasion of 1814.

Saving the National Treasures

When the Battle of Bladensburg began, President Madison and other officials fled Washington, D.C., to nearby Georgetown. As the British approached the capital, First Lady Dolley Madison refused to leave until she had packed up a prized portrait of George Washington and a copy of the Declaration of Independence. With those items safe, she escaped, leaving her own possessions behind. That evening, while British soldiers ransacked the president's mansion and the capital burned, the president and his wife found each other among crowds and chaos in Georgetown.

Chapter Three

Attack on Fort McHenry

The British set fires all over Washington, D.C., in August 1814. The city burned for two days.

The Capture of William Beanes

The destruction of Washington, D.C., continued for two more days in August 1814. Huge fires burned across the city, and flames were visible 50 miles (80 km) away in Baltimore. On August 26, as the British withdrew to ships on the Potomac River, they took a prisoner named William Beanes, a doctor.

On August 30, a local militia officer, Francis Scott Key, learned of the capture of his friend Beanes. He persuaded

Settling Differences
"All our differences with the Yankees will be shortly settled. This war cannot last long."

British commander General Robert Ross, in a letter to his wife, September 10, 1814

Colonel John Skinner, the U.S. government official in charge of prisoner negotiations, to sail down Chesapeake Bay to meet the British fleet and negotiate Beanes' release. On September 3, the two men set off in a **sloop**.

The British Plan for Baltimore

The large British fleet, meanwhile, was sailing up the bay toward Baltimore. On September 7, Key and Skinner met the British commanders, General Robert Ross and Admiral George Cockburn. Key and Skinner showed them letters from wounded British prisoners, thanking Dr. Beanes for the care he had given them.

The British officers agreed to release Beanes, but they would not permit the three Americans to leave right away because the men had learned too much about the plan for the attack on Baltimore. They were placed under guard on their boat behind the British fleet to wait out the battle.

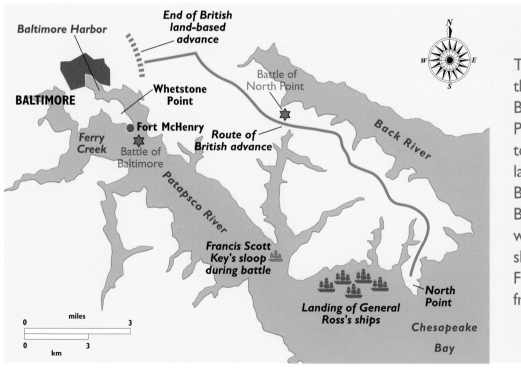

This map shows the sites of the Battle of North Point, which took place on land, and the Battle of Baltimore, in which British ships attacked Fort McHenry from the water.

Fort McHenry

Fort McHenry was originally built as Fort Whetstone in 1776, during the American Revolution. Whetstone Point, where the fort stood, was surrounded on three sides by water. Any ship sailing into Baltimore Harbor would have no choice but to pass by the fort's guns.

The star-shaped, stone structure that stands today was started in 1798 and finished in 1803. It was renamed Fort McHenry in honor of former secretary of war James McHenry. (McHenry's son, also named James, was an **artillery** officer at the fort during the battle in 1814.)

When the War of 1812 began, new guns and cannons were added to the fort. The army also built hot shot furnaces, large brick ovens that heated cannonballs until they were red-hot. The cannonballs were then fired from the fort's cannons at enemy ships during battles.

The British Plan

The British plan was to land several thousand men on North Point, a **peninsula** south of the city. The soldiers would invade Baltimore, but not until British warships had bombarded Fort McHenry.

The Battle of North Point

On September 12, 1814, more than five thousand British troops landed at North Point and began the march northwest

18

British commander General Robert Ross is shot at the beginning of the Battle of North Point.

toward Baltimore. They soon encountered a small force of Americans who opened fire from the woods. When General Ross rode to the front of the march to see what was causing the delay, he was shot and killed. The death of Ross was a bad start for the British.

The British pressed forward until they once again met enemy forces in the Battle of North Point. After a short but intense fight, the Americans retreated. The British forces, however, suffered almost 350 **casualties**. They decided to stop and set up camp for the night and wait for the attack on Fort McHenry to begin.

Treacherous Waters

The British ships also had problems. The water around Fort McHenry was too shallow to permit the largest British ships to come close enough to fire on the fort. Admiral Cockburn was forced to attack Fort McHenry with a reduced fleet of sixteen warships, ten of which were small gun ships.

Heading for Battle

"For the first time in my life I took my musket and entered a regiment and headed for battle."

Nineteen-year-old U.S. Army private Martin Gillette, describing how he went to fight the British at North Point

19

This 1816 print by J. Bower shows the British bombardment of Fort McHenry.

The British Open Fire

Shortly after sunrise on September 13, the British opened fire on Fort McHenry to begin the Battle of Baltimore. Inside the fort were about one thousand men under the command of Major George Armistead. From 2 miles (3 km) away, the British warships fired cannonballs, **Congreve rockets**, and **mortar rounds**. Throughout the morning, the British fired more than one shot a minute at the fort. Luckily, most shells landed harmlessly because the British fire was inaccurate.

The Land Forces Give Up

The land-based British troops, meanwhile, heard the attack and advanced toward Baltimore again. On the way, they met a huge force of Maryland militia that was dug in behind **fortifications** on high ground. The British troops tried to get around the militia, but the militia fought them off. Later that night, the British gave up and returned to North Point.

The Long Bombardment

In the afternoon of September 13, Admiral Cockburn ordered his ships to close in on Fort McHenry. Finally, the British ships were in range of the fort's cannons. As they got closer, the British ships were struck with intense fire from the fort. Cockburn immediately retreated and resumed the long-range attack.

The Attack Fails

For twenty-five hours, as lightning flashed and rain fell, the British bombarded the fort. But the Americans inside stood their ground. By dawn, the British officers realized that the attack on Baltimore would fail. At about 7:00 A.M. on September 14, the British ceased their attack on Fort McHenry. The Battle of Baltimore was over.

Few Losses

"The bombardment continued . . . until 7 o'clock on Wednesday morning . . . [about] 25 hours with . . . 15 to 1800 shells . . . thrown by the enemy. A large proportion burst over us . . . and about 400 fell within the works. . . . I am happy to inform you (wonderful as it may appear) that our loss amounts only to four men killed, and 24 wounded."

Major George Armistead, battle report written September 24, 1814

Cannons perch on the walls of Fort McHenry today. When the British moved in close on September 13, the cannons fired at the attacking ships.

Francis Scott Key (1779–1843)

Francis Scott Key was born in the western Maryland town of Frederick. He graduated from St. John's College in Annapolis at age seventeen, and by 1805 he had become a lawyer in Georgetown, Maryland. Key was deeply involved in the Episcopal Church in his town. As a **pacifist**, he opposed all wars. When the British sailed into Chesapeake Bay, however, Key volunteered to serve in the Georgetown Light Field Artillery militia unit. After the War of 1812 ended, Key served as a U.S. District Attorney. He also wrote several hymns. He died on January 11, 1843, and was buried at Mount Olivet Cemetery in Frederick, Maryland. The U.S. flag flies over his tomb night and day, as it does at Fort McHenry.

When Francis Scott Key (center) caught sight of the Star-Spangled Banner, he realized that Fort McHenry had not surrendered to the British in spite of the long bombardment.

This is the first verse of Key's poem "The Defense of Fort McHenry." It is the earliest of Key's handwritten drafts known to be in existence.

The Sight of the Flag

Down river, Francis Scott Key and his two companions had heard the thunderous barrage and imagined the worst for the U.S. defenders at Fort McHenry. But as his freed sloop sailed up the Patapsco River, Key saw an enormous U.S. flag flying over the fort. He began to write the words that would make him famous.

On September 17, 1814, Key's poem, "The Defense of Fort McHenry," was published. The poem immediately became so popular that its words were set to the music of a popular British song, "To Anacreon in Heaven." The result was the song known today as "The Star-Spangled Banner."

The Star-Spangled Banner

"Oh, say can you see, by the dawn's early light,
What so proudly we hailed at the twilight's last gleaming?
Whose broad stripes and bright stars, through
the perilous fight,
O'er the ramparts we watched, were so gallantly streaming?
And the rockets' red glare, the bombs bursting in air,
Gave proof through the night that our flag was still there.
O say, does that star-spangled banner yet wave
O'er the land of the free and the home of the brave?"

*Francis Scott Key, first verse of "The Defense
of Fort McHenry," 1814*

Chapter Four

The Final Months

A news bulletin, published in Boston in February 1815, announced that a peace treaty had been signed, ending the War of 1812.

A Peace Mission

While the Battle of Baltimore was unfolding, U.S. officials were sailing to Ghent, in Belgium, to begin peace negotiations with Britain. They had left several weeks before Washington, D.C., was attacked, and they had no idea what was happening in the United States as they sailed across the Atlantic.

The Americans were on a peace mission because the main issues that sparked the War of 1812 no longer existed. The British had stopped interfering with U.S. shipping and were no longer impressing American sailors.

The Treaty of Ghent

The two sides argued for months over the peace treaty. The United States refused to sign until the British agreed to withdraw from U.S. territory in the Northwest. The British eventually agreed, and the Treaty of Ghent was signed on December 24, 1814. In the end, the peace treaty did not give the two nations anything more than they had to begin with, and it addressed none of the problems that had caused the war in the first place.

Evening Gazette Office,

Boston, Monday, 10, A.M.

The following most highly important handbill has just been issued from the Centinel press. We deem a duty that we owe our Friends and the Public to assist in the prompt spread of the Glorious News.

Treaty of PEACE signed and arrived.

Centinel Office, Feb. 13, 1815, 8 o'clock in the morning.

WE have this instant received in Thirty-two hours from New-York the following

Great and Happy News!
FOR THE PUBLIC.

To Benjamin Russell, Esq. Centinel-Office, Boston.
New-York, Feb. 11, 1815—Saturday Evening, 10 o'clock.

SIR—

I HASTEN to acquaint you, for the information of the Public, of the arrival here this afternoon of H. Br. M. sloop of war *Favorite*, in which has come passenger Mr Carroll, American Messenger, having in his possession

A Treaty of Peace

Between this Country and Great-Britain, signed on the 26th December last.

Mr Baker also is on board, as Agent for the British Government, the same who was formerly Charge des Affairs here.

Mr Carroll reached town at eight o'clock this evening. He shewed to a friend of mine, who is acquainted with him, the packet containing the *Treaty*, and a London newspaper of the last date of December, announcing the signing of the Treaty.

It depends, however, as my friend observed, upon the act of the President to suspend hostilities on this side.

The gentleman left London the 2d Jan. The *Transit* had sailed previously from a port on the Continent.

This city is in a perfect uproar of joy, shouts, illuminations, &c. &c.

I have undertaken to send you this by Express—the rider engaging to deliver it by Eight o'clock on Monday morning. The expense will be 225 dollars.—If you can collect so much to indemnify me I will thank you to do so.

I am with respect, Sir, your obedient servant,

JONATHAN GOODHUE.

We most ardently felicitate our Country on this auspicious news, which may be relied on as wholly authentic.—Centinel.

PEACE EXTRA.

The Battle of New Orleans

Communication was very slow across the Atlantic, and news of the Treaty of Ghent took weeks to reach the United States. The lack of communication led to one final battle being fought after the treaty was signed. It was, in fact, the largest battle of the war. In January 1815, General Andrew Jackson of the U.S. Army turned back an attack by British forces at the Battle of New Orleans. The British suffered more than two thousand casualties, while the Americans lost fewer than a hundred men. When Congress approved the Treaty of Ghent on February 17, 1815—following the major victory at New Orleans—many Americans thought the United States had defeated Britain. In truth, neither side had won the war.

U.S. forces push back the British in the Battle of New Orleans. It was the last battle of the War of 1812.

A Shocking Sight

"Of all the sights I ever witnessed, that . . . was . . . the most shocking. Within . . . a few hundred yards were gathered together nearly a thousand bodies, all of them arrayed in British uniforms. Not a single American was among them; all were English; and they were thrown by dozens into shallow holes, scarcely deep enough to furnish them with a slight covering of earth."

British officer George Gleig, describing the scene after the Battle of New Orleans, the last battle of the War of 1812, January 1815

Conclusion

Visitors to Fort McHenry can walk around the fortifications, imagining what it would have been like to be there during the battle nearly two hundred years ago.

A National Song

"The Star-Spangled Banner" became enormously popular in the years immediately after its publication. It was one of the favorite songs of Union troops during the Civil War. In 1931, Congress officially named "The Star-Spangled Banner" as the national anthem of the United States.

Fort McHenry Today

After the War of 1812, Fort McHenry was never attacked again, but it continued to play a part in defending the United States. It was used for training soldiers in the Mexican War of 1846–1848 and to house Confederate prisoners during the Civil War of 1861–1865. The military left Fort McHenry in 1912, and it became a hospital shortly afterward.

Fort McHenry was taken over by the National Park Service in 1933. As a national monument and the National Park Service's only historic shrine, it is visited by thousands of people every year.

This is the flag that flew over Fort McHenry in 1814, the original Star-Spangled Banner.

The Star-Spangled Banner

In June 1813, when Major George Armistead took command of Fort McHenry, he wrote a letter to the commander of the Baltimore militia. It read, "We, Sir, are ready at Fort McHenry to defend Baltimore against invading by the enemy. That is to say, we are ready except that we have no suitable ensign to display over the Star Fort, and it is my desire to have a flag so large that the British will have no difficulty in seeing it from a distance."

Mary Young Pickersgill, with help from her daughter and two nieces, began work on a huge flag. The flag measures 42 by 30 feet (13 by 9 meters)—about one-quarter the size of a basketball court. Each of the flag's fifteen stars is two feet (0.6 m) across. The Star-Spangled Banner is now at the National Museum of American History in Washington, D.C.

Time Line

1793	Napoleonic Wars begin.
1803	Louisiana Purchase.
1803–1812	British navy impresses more than ten thousand U.S. sailors.
1807	June: Three Americans are killed and eighteen wounded when USS *Chesapeake* is fired upon by British warship *Leopard*.
	December 22: Embargo Act becomes law.
1809	Embargo Act is repealed.
	James Madison becomes U.S. president.
1811	War Hawks press for invasion of Canada.
1812	June 18: U.S. Congress declares war on Britain.
	British capture U.S. forts in the West.
1813	April 27: Battle of York.
	September 10: Battle of Lake Erie.
	October 15: Tecumseh is killed at Battle of the Thames.
1814	August 24: Battle of Bladensburg.
	August 24–25: Washington, D.C., is burned by British forces.
	September 12: Battle of North Point.
	September 13–14: U.S. forces defend Fort McHenry in Battle of Baltimore.
	September 17: Francis Scott Key's poem, "The Defense of Fort McHenry," is published.
	December 24: British and U.S. diplomats sign Treaty of Ghent in Belgium.
1815	January 8: U.S. forces defeat British army at Battle of New Orleans.
	February 17: Treaty of Ghent is approved by United States.
1931	"The Star-Spangled Banner" is adopted as U.S. national anthem.
1933	Fort McHenry is taken over by National Park Service.

Things to Think About and Do

A Poem for an Important Event
In 1814, Francis Scott Key wrote his poem, "The Defense of Fort Henry," because he was inspired by an important event. Think of another important and inspiring event in your nation's history and write a poem about it.

Embargo
Today, the United States still places restrictions on trade with certain nations, as it did before the War of 1812. Find out what you can about embargoes in place today and the reasons for them. What are the problems caused by such restrictions? What are the advantages for the United States?

Inside Fort McHenry
Imagine you are a soldier inside Fort McHenry when the British bombardment begins in September 1814. Write a journal entry for three days: the day before the attack, the day of the battle, and the day of the ceasefire.

Glossary

artillery:	large, heavy guns such as cannons.
blockade:	blocking off of a port using ships to prevent the enemy from going in or out.
casualty:	soldier or other person who is killed, wounded, or missing in battle.
confederation:	alliance of groups that agree to act together and support each other.
Congreve rocket:	self-propelled missile carrying explosives.
economy:	system of producing and distributing goods and services.
embargo:	ban on trade and transport of goods between one country and another.
fleet:	group of ships under a single command.
fortification:	structure built to defend a place or to strengthen an existing structure.
merchant ship:	ship carrying cargo of goods to be sold.
militia:	group of citizens organized into an unofficial army.
mortar round:	shell or other object fired from a mortar, which is a type of cannon.
Northwest:	part of the West in the early 1800s that was north of the Ohio River, now comprising the states of Wisconsin, Michigan, Illinois, Indiana, and Ohio.
pacifist:	person who opposes war even if his or her country is attacked.
peninsula:	piece of land jutting out into water but connected to mainland.
repeal:	undo an earlier decision or law.
shell:	case that contains explosives and is fired from a gun.
sloop:	small, single-masted sailing vessel.
West:	area of North America in the early 1800s between the original U.S. states and the Mississippi River.

Further Information

Books

Fitterer, C. Ann. *Tecumseh: Chief of the Shawnee* (Our People). Child's World, 2002.

Gregson, Susan R. *Francis Scott Key: Patriotic Poet*. Bridgestone, 2003.

Maynard, Charles W. *Fort McHenry* (Famous Forts Throughout American History). Powerkids Press, 2003.

Quiri, Patricia Ryon. *The National Anthem*. Children's Press, 1998.

Santella, Andrew. *War of 1812* (Cornerstones of Freedom). Scholastic, 2000.

Web Sites

www.americanhistory.si.edu/ssb The National Museum of American History, which houses the Star-Spangled Banner, has an online exhibition all about the flag, its history, and its restoration.

www.nps.gov/fomc The National Park Service's web site gives information about Fort McHenry National Monument, together with historical information and maps of the fort.

www.warof1812.ca Canadian military heritage web site has documents, video clips, and articles about the War of 1812.

Useful Addresses

Fort McHenry National Monument and Historic Shrine
National Park Service
End of East Fort Avenue
Baltimore, MD 21230
Telephone: (410) 962-4290

Index